FOOL'S PA

Zoe Brooks

Black Eyes Publishing UK

FOOL'S PARADISE
By Zoe Brooks
© Zoe Brooks 1992, 2022

Published in 2022
Black Eyes Publishing UK
50 Boverton Drive
Brockworth, Gloucester
GL3 4DA (UK)

www.blackeyespublishinguk.co.uk

ISBN: 978-1-913195-19-9

Previously published by
White Fox Books
ISBN 978-0-9572341-0-9
(Electronic Book Text)

Edited by: Josephine Lay

Cover Painting: Hannah Kodicek

Cover design: Jason Conway, The Daydream Academy.
www.thedaydreamacademy.com

Fool's Paradise was first performed at Vauxhall St Peter's Heritage Centre, Kennington Lane, London SE11 1992.

Sections of Fool's Paradise were first published in *Aquarius Women* 1992.

FOOL'S PARADISE

A poem for voices.

CONTENTS

PART ONE – A BEGINNING

Traveller 1   Where begins the hard road, the long road
the dark road?
Where begins the road of sharp stones
of bare feet, of blood on the stones
and the grass like saw teeth?

Traveller 2   Between two rocks at a crossroads,
where the gibbet drips bones
and the sky is grey and heavy
and the curtain is not rent
and the hand of God is indiscernible
and the breath of God is fiery
upon the bare heads of the people
there begins the road.

Traveller 3   At that crossroads
they have placed a circle of melted candles,
with photographs made a shrine.

Traveller 1&3   We come bearing the stamp of empire,
the drip, drip, drip of power.
They come bearing the ashes of martyrs
dark the stains on the square.

Traveller 1   We will walk the road together
a little while, I think.

Traveller 2   Here in the square our heads
are light with caffeine

and the tongues of birds.

Fool	Like a rook I perch on one leg.
I twist my head to one side
so that my ear touches my shoulder.
I close one eye.
Upon the road there are three travellers.
Two wear the clothes of passage,
one the garb of a defrocked priest.

Welcome gentlemen, ladies.
I will gather your shadows
and take them to be cleaned.
I will lay them on the flat stones of the river
and beat the shit out of them.
Forgive my language, but I believe in accuracy.

Traveller 1	You are welcome to them.

Fool	They will be returned as grey as new.
In the interim, sit upon these stones
and mark the sun,
so that the laying out of the shadows
does not go amiss.

Traveller 3	We will.

Fool	My dog will entertain you.
If you have a bishop's hat amongst you
he will fly at it and worry it
until it cries "Amen".

Traveller 1	Please take care of them. Mine I bought in Damascus, there can be no shadow finer.
Traveller 2	Why do you pander to this fool? Shadows indeed!
Traveller 1	We are strangers in a strange country. Even you, who was born here cannot find the way.
Traveller 3	What good are a child's memories of familiar places, when all is grown unfamiliar?
Fool	Gentlemen, ladies, sit and I will cut your feet free. Your tongues I will cut later.
Traveller 2	This is ridiculous.
Traveller 3	Be still.
Traveller 1	I've heard it said that the devil sometimes comes in the form of a black dog.
Traveller 2	I've heard that too.
Traveller 3	I know it.
Traveller 1	That he capers for sticks

and pursues his tail
round and around
the devil caught in a hell
of his own making.

Traveller 2   I'd heard that it was because
the doctor left a corner of the pentagram open,
and through the open angle
his power drained like sand in an hourglass
on to the floor,
where he rolled to kill the fleas.

Traveller 3   I saw him once at the door.

Traveller 2   What?

Traveller 3   I saw him – huge, black –
not a poodle at all.
His eyes were bigger than himself,
and his jaws were red,
and from his teeth saliva like maggots.
He was knocking at the door,
with his whole body knocking.

Traveller 1   "This ae nighte, this ae nighte,
(singing)   every nighte and alle,
fire and sleet and candlelighte
and Christe receive thy soule.
When thou from hence away art past,
every nighte and alle,
to Whinny-muir thou comst at last
and Christe receive thy soule."

Traveller 3	"From Whinny-muir to Brig O'Dread,
	from Brig O'Dread to Purgatory Fire
	thou comst at last.
	And Christe receive thy soule."
Traveller 1	I'd forgotten the old song.
	Just came to me.
	Never understood it really.
Traveller 3	What is this place?
Traveller 2	Have you got the map?
	There's a river down there,
	with a narrow bridge.
	Beside it our mottled friend
	is savagely beating the shadows.
	Look there,
	through the bushes at the water's edge
	rides a horseman – a militiaman –
	with polished black boots
	and peaked hat shading his eyes.
	At his side a sword hilt glistens.
	Through the shallows the painted hooves
	stir up mud and small shrimps.
	Up the steep path and over the bridge.
	He doesn't acknowledge the laundryman,
	he is thinking of cool beer and warm guns.
	The laundryman doesn't look up,
	but starts his work again,
	washing away the shrimps and mud.

Traveller 1   Before we go any further
you must answer this question:
who are you?

Fool   Never rock the cradle
while the baby is asleep,
nor beat the dog while it's hunting.
Never hold kittens in soiled hands,
nor say to a woman
that she may love neither God nor man.
But enough of me,
did you see our visitor?

Traveller 2   Yes.

Fool   He was measuring up your shadows for chains.
But do not fear, the sun was low.
For him you are giants, gentlemen.

Traveller 2   So at last you have noticed
there are no ladies present.

Fool   Not now that fear is in the company.

❧

Traveller 2   See how the dog always prances
one step behind our guide,
leaping up,
catching at the man's tattered coat,

urging like an Italian dance master
the raising of the knees.

Traveller 3   No, you are wrong.
When the sun is behind
he runs in front,
when in front behind,
and when it is noon
he weaves in and out
of his master's legs.

Traveller 1   And at night?

Traveller 3   He hides from the moon,
I have watched him.

Traveller 1   A wise dog with a foolish master.

Traveller 3   You think so?

Traveller 2   We are all fools here,
we do not speak his language.

Traveller 1   I looked for food,
but on the thorn
the berries are covered
with fine white mould.

Fool   These lands are man-made.
        No good can come of them.

Traveller 2   The hills of slate and limestone
        are bare of grass.
        In the hollow is a pond,
        a wash pool for sheep
        by the looks of it.
        The tadpoles are bubbling
        at the water's edge.

Fool   Ignore them.
        Ignore the fish in the brown waters,
        ignore the huntsman's mound at the quarry
        brow,
        ignore the orchids like insects.
        We won't waste time here.
        Where man has torn out the heart of stone
        there's no staying.
        Do not blunder into the long sharp grass,
        the serpent waits there for voles.

Traveller 2   What is that bell?

Fool   There is a church in the trees,
        the bell calls the monks from the valley –
        the bowl waits the letting of blood.
        Soon we will hear them singing,
        as they gather wolf's bane and dogwort.
        But now is not the time to shake the empty hand.
        There's no food here.

∞

Traveller 3	Sometimes the Fool walks
	as if his clothes
	have invented his body,
	as if each movement
	is a fabrication of folds;
	and from his head a thread
	falls straight as a plumb-line
	into the centre of the earth.
	I sometimes think
	I could seize his hand, his arm,
	his shoulder
	and holding them tightly
	bundle them up,
	tie them in a knot
	like old sheets
	and place him on my back.
	Wishful thinking, probably.
Traveller 2	I don't know, possibly.
	Listening to you
	I find myself thinking
	of the old ordnance maps.
	You know the ones –
	the ones reinforced with fabric?
	Maybe not.
	Perhaps your country
	was never mapped
	for target practice,
	your timetables never structured

for the movement of troops.

Traveller 3   What are you saying?
That the fool is a creation of guns?

Traveller 2   Yes, maybe.
And maybe that he is our way out.

Traveller 1   In, more like.

ৡৰ৶

Fool   What am I?
Don't you know?
I am a puppet master.

Traveller 1   And from his sack
he took a sheep's skull,
with his thumb wedged in the jaw
and two fingers looped
through the eye sockets.

Fool   May I introduce my friend – Punch?

Traveller 2   That's not –

Fool   Not as he was – no.
Not with his tassels and bells,
nor his bright red clothes.
But now –

Traveller 1	Does he speak?
Traveller 2	Go on! When I was a kid I used to love that voice of his.
Fool	Not any more – the dogs are playing with his tongue down in the Badlands. One day he walked too close to the wire. For a while he chattered, cursed, shook his tiny fist, but the hangmen in their white coats and gardeners' gloves tore out his tongue and threw it away. As for the rest of his flesh there was no use for it.
Traveller 2	No, it can't be! You're lying. No one can kill him, not even the devil. I know the story by heart, "Put your head in here – Punch."
Traveller 3	"What in there?"
Traveller 2	"No."
Traveller 3	"In there?"
Traveller 2	"No."

Traveller 3	"Well, where then?"
Traveller 2	"In the noose."
Traveller 3	"In the juice?"
Traveller 2	"No!"
Traveller 3	"In the sluice?"
Traveller 2	"No, come here I'll show you – aargh!"
Fool	Sentimentality for murderers, that's all that saved him then. But Judy will not intercede for him, he has no Margareta.

ॐ

Traveller 2	The sun is low, the sky is taut grey, Peregrine paeonies lift up their cupped hands.
Traveller 3	Look, see where the grey opens to reveal cumulus clouds high above, made pink by the setting sun, like two halves of a brain – melting, mounting, forming.

Traveller 2	We watch.
Fool	You look up. Do you think he is there? Your way is down.
	Now we only walk on the brim of the world. Mayfly larvae must struggle in the mud before they break through the skin and stand upon the concave world a while.
	Come, my little grubs, allusions over. We are expected.
Traveller 2	Who expects us?
Fool	No one that is not here already.
Traveller 2	You're talking gobbledegook as usual.
Fool	Possibly, as usual. But that is not my problem, I say only what I am meant to say.

჻

Fool	At my father's house I am the keeper of the garden. I sweep up the leaves, rake the branches from the lake.

In summer when the roses are blown
I behead them and bury their beauty
in precious oils.
And with each knife cut
the sap runs like blood.

It is my duty to make the first cut,
to graft and to tie,
to smear the wounds with mud.
And it is I who tears out the suckers,
the strong green suckers
of the stronger parent plant.

For I bind my hands with leather thongs,
as my father once did,
to guard against the thorn.
And I do not hear the scream of the sap,
of the epidermis, of the pith and cortex.
I am become accustomed
to the brown smell of mould,
to the flexing of the worm on the fork.
I have dug in the dark ground for roots.

PART TWO – CITY AND TRIAL

Traveller 1   Where have all these people come from?

Traveller 3   Why do they walk in the shadow
of the castle walls?

Traveller 1   By the slow river
with its weirs and dying swans,
in the long shadow of the castle gates,
the people walk.
We look about us like idiots,
lolling our heads from side to side.
"Shall fires never make us shrink?
We gave neither food nor drink."

Traveller 3   They do not look at us.

Traveller 1   They look ahead – solidly ahead –
women, children and men
bare their heads
and move their lips.

Traveller 2   What are we doing here?
It is dangerous to walk with them –
these quiet people with eyes of fire.
Haven't they seen the phial of acid?

Traveller 3   Some of them
are now carrying banners.

Traveller 2   My God! I know them.
I carried them once.
But I was too much a coward
to carry the banner and the card.
I fled,
burning one and leaving the other.

Traveller 3   This is ludicrous.
What was the Fool doing
to leave us here?
Your memories
are dangerous, my friend,
I fear, I fear.

Another voice   The castle walls will blow.
Shout and we will bring them down.

Traveller 2   The bomb is in the flowerbed.
How did I know that?
Why did I say it?

Another voice   Shout!

Voices   Yes!

Traveller 2   A cloud of dust and masonry
rocks the castle wall.
Within my inside pocket
near my heart
I feel the thin glass tube
where my passport used to be.
Reaching in

I take out a glass phial
barely two inches long
but with enough clear liquid
within to turn a face to ash.
Jesus, forgive me!

Fool   "The fire will burn thee to the bare bane
(singing)   and Christe receive thy soule.
This ae nighte, this ae nighte
every nighte and alle.
Fire and sleet and candle lighte
and Christe receive thy soule."

Traveller 1   Wake up – you are dreaming, friend.

Traveller 3   It is nothing but a nightmare.

Traveller 2   What? A nightmare,
ah yes.
I was dreaming of a woman
not quite in her prime
sitting in front
of a dressing-room mirror.
In the glare of the light bulbs
she was removing white make-up.
And a man
reached over her bare shoulder
and laid upon the dressing table
a glass test tube with black stopper.
I saw only his arm.
He was in shadow,

but I felt his breath
on her shoulder as he said,
"Sometimes it is best to miss a cue.
Words are dangerous.
You know what this can do."

༄

Traveller 1	I have lost it!
Traveller 3	What's the matter?
Traveller 1	I've lost it –
Traveller 2	What?
Traveller 1	Something – nothing. I carried it all this way in my sack, all the way from the city of angels.
Traveller 3	What was it? We will help you look.
Traveller 1	I said it was nothing. Well, nothing much – a pad of paper, cost me sixty crowns. There, I said it was nothing.

Traveller 3	We can buy some more.
Traveller 1	No, it won't do.
Traveller 2	Have you written something on it? Is that it?
Traveller 1	Yes – but that's not it. I have kept my writings. It's the paper I'm missing. I need it.
Traveller 2	What was so special?
Traveller 1	It had a grain and lines a centimetre apart – fudged blue lines badly printed on badly made paper. It was my pad of paper that's all.
Traveller 2	I don't see your problem. We'll get some more – smooth as silk.
Traveller 3	So smooth a woman could wear it.
Traveller 2	Smooth enough for you to deface it with pride.
Traveller 1	No! It was my talisman.

Whilst I had it
I could mount each blue line.
It was my ladder out.
Don't you see?
My stairs back to the angels,
and now I have lost it
and I am lost too.

Traveller 2   We have the map.

Traveller 3   Damn your map!
Do you think it means anything here?
All it is – is a disguise,
a disguise for blank paper.
You pretend you know this place –
with your compass
and emigré-returns stare.
You say you know the tongue.
But you are as lost as anyone here.
Where are we going?
Answer me that.
The Fool slipped upon his own words
when he said he'd cut our tongues.
Oh, he was so sharp
he cut himself in the carving.
But not before he slashed our mouths
and turned our gibberish
into anger and fear.

Traveller 2   A cat carries a dead bird,
                   limp as a kitten,
                   over the tram lines to the centre
                   of the road.
                   There it sets down the bundle
                   and begins to mew
                   loud, sharp in the early morning air.
                   A solitary car stops
                   as the cat mourns and pleads
                   for the game to start again.
                   Half proud, half defensive,
                   it ignores the engine's low growl.
                   Around the corner comes the clang
                   of a tram two cars long;
                   the cat responding to the bell
                   picks up its prize
                   and just quick enough
                   to avoid the trolley wheels
                   stalks under the parked cars' arches
                   and on to the pavement.

Traveller 1   In the doorway
                   where the cat lays out its prize
                   a man felled by indiscriminate age
                   lies sleeping,
                   curled as vagrants do against the cold.
                   His worn soles appear
                   from beneath an army greatcoat,
                   his unwashed hair,
                   covered by newspaper,
                   his fingers cupped to make a pillow.

The cat curls into the hollow
between his knees and chest
and sleeps too.

ೲ

Traveller 2	The guidebook says that we can get the key from the janitor.
Traveller 1	Is it worth it?
Traveller 2	Yes, yes. This church is very special to me, I want you to see it.
Traveller 3	It's in the middle of a slum. We had quite a trip coming here and not one to be taken lightly – the wooden slatted houses like those in shadow shows, the open sewer – very pretty indeed!
Traveller 1	And where is this janitor?
Child	You want to go in sir?
Traveller 2	Yes.
Child	I'll get my mother, stay here.

Traveller 3	Why did you give him a tip? We'll see no more of him!
Traveller 2	I hear with my little ear something sounding like "lane".
Traveller 1	Train?
Traveller 2	No.
Traveller 1	Plain?
Traveller 3	Skein?
Traveller 1	Pain? Blame?
Traveller 2	Nowhere near.
Traveller 3	Refrain?
Traveller 2	No.
Traveller 1	Restrain?
Traveller 2	Close.
Traveller 1	Rain?
Traveller 2	Cold.
Traveller 1	Bane? Disdain?

Traveller 2   You've got it.

Traveller 3   Disdain?
You hear disdain? Where?

Traveller 2   Everywhere
in your tortured vowels, friend.
This is my country.
Those wooden houses are my houses,
that child, my child.
It was your country which sold mine
for a few years' peace.
If that is an open drain
you have shat in it
and made our waters foul.

Woman   My son tells me you want to see the church.

Traveller 1   Yes, yes, we do.
You have the key?

Woman   Of course, I am its guardian.
The door is heavy
and the hinges rusty,
but if now you put your shoulders to it
you will find the door unlocked.

Traveller 1   We put our shoulders to the door
and just as our feet
begin to slip on the gravel
the door swings open.

The dust of centuries
spirals in the incoming sunshine.
We enter, stop, allow our eyes to adjust.

Traveller 3 The woman sits on a wooden chair
by the door and waits.

Traveller 1 The church has a smell
of decaying books.
From the walls hang army banners,
grown thin as lace.

Traveller 3 He leads us
through the arch into the nave.
At one end across the whole wall
is a fresco of the Last Day.

Traveller 1 The dead are torn from their graves
by Christ bestride the world.
At his feet are a set of scales
manned by devils and angels.
The jaws of Hell brush his sandals.
Already the bellows are working,
keys and tongs litter the hot ground.

One devil stirs a large pot
with a kitchen ladle,
another turns a roasting rack
and cuts a sliver
from a well-done thigh.
Above Christ's head the angels
are in their glory

but we are watching the other place
in its domesticity of terror.

Traveller 3   Our guide leads us away from Hell
and up the nave
made narrow by rubble.

Traveller 1   In the great dome above our heads
The Pantocrator sits in judgement
his forearm and hand raised
against the gold firmament,
his crown – the cross.

Traveller 3   But we are led
through a small doorway to our left.
Here in a side chapel, we stop.

Traveller 1   The whole place
is liquid with gold light,
a gold richer
than that which shone in the dome,
richer still than the thin threads
running through
the moth-eaten banners.

Traveller 3   The light falls through
yellow stained-glass windows,
which are recessed
into the thick stone walls.

Traveller 1   We do not look at them,
but instead,

in the centre of the light,
our eyes are drawn to a pietà
– a simple stone pietà.
Christ's limbs have been stretched
by the weight of the body,
the head hangs back,
the thorns are slipping,
the jaw is set in pain.

Traveller 3   In death his pain is unending.

Traveller 1   The mother's arms
hang loosely by her side.
What good is cradling now?

Woman   It is very fine, I think.

Traveller 1   Yes.

Woman   And very sad. You see the flowers?

Traveller 3   All about the low statue
are small bunches of flowers.
Many are tied with ribbons,
nearly all are brown and crumbling.
Their scent had struck us
when first we came into the church.

Woman   The mothers used to come here
when their sons were taken.
They'd come, leave a gift and pray.
And then,

when there was nothing left to do,
they'd cross themselves and leave.
Each bunch of flowers is a man's life.
There isn't a family in the city
that hasn't cause to come here.

Traveller 1   How did you come to be its guardian?

Woman   I do not know –
I was an actress once,
not a very good one, perhaps,
but an actress.

Traveller 2   Why do you say that?
You were the best and you know it.

Traveller 3   She smiles and looks at him.

Woman   Are you still in the land of the living?

Traveller 2   She says and shifts my bones.

Woman   Are you coming up for air?

Traveller 1   Things become unclear.

Traveller 2   The ossuary is full tonight,
they're hanging from the rafters.
They're piling up flowers and candle wax,
charcoaled bones and onion skins,
prayers, offertory cakes and ale.

Traveller 3	Why does my mouth feel full of clay?
Traveller 1	This was so logical, so reasoned – but now there is nothing to hold on to.
Woman	But dreams.
Traveller 1	But dreams.
Traveller 2	The electric razor in the corner flashes as it recharges. I did not know her: she has shaved her head.
Woman	My little ones, my darling ones, my dears.
Traveller 3	We knock against the sky like dead men.
Woman	"Here comes a candle to light you to bed."
Traveller 2	"And here comes a chopper to chop off –"
Traveller 1	"Your head."
Traveller 3	This is one hell of a church you've brought us to.
Traveller 1	And who is your avenging angel – your actress friend –

who cradles Christ upon her breast
and straightens his long fingers
again, and again in vain,
for the tendon is severed
by the nail.
This hand will not rise to the heavens
in judgement,
will bear only the mother's tears.
We dare not look
into her secret eyes, no one dares.

Traveller 2   Mother do not weep for me,
who am in the grave.

Traveller 3   Our faces and our voices fall apart.

಄಄

Man   You stand falsely accused
that on the day after Candlemas
you did bring outlanders
through the hidden pathways,
that on this and other occasions
you did call your dog "Lazarus"
and set him to fly at bishops' caps.

You stand falsely accused
that you did hide
from the guardians of the bridge
and washed dirt

from the soles of strangers,
that you gathered cobwebs
from the doorways of officials
and cleared snail shells from pathways.

You stand falsely accused
that you did dance lovely on the water,
that you are the breath of methane
and thrice the cock denied you.
You stand falsely accused
that you are the show of cattle
that you are the afterbirth
and the heaving.

You stand falsely accused
that on Sunday last
you did move upon the face of the waters,
and as you did
you whistled down the wind.

You stand falsely accused
that you did steal the throats of birds
and placed milk upon the housewife's lips.
That you did upon such and such a day
destroy the fabric of the world
and wore a hat of many colours.

You stand falsely accused
that you were whipped
through the streets of Ninevah
for bringing the town into ill repute,
that you slept with whores

and did no more than sleep,
that your bedstead is made of brass
and your house upon sand.

You stand falsely accused
that you slit the membrane
that binds the tongue-tied,
that you peeped through the shutters
and wakened the town.

You stand falsely accused
that you deserve nothing better,
that your socks need darning,
that you did reeve the winds to the mast
and wished the sailors "Bon voyage",
that all the snowballs in Hell
could not wash your underwear,
that women despair of you
and the old cry out to you in the street.

You stand falsely accused
of ordering more wine on a Sabbath,
of gilding lilies
and tending fallen swine.
You stand falsely accused
of knotting wood,
of throwing pots
and firing blanks.

You are falsely accused
of coming into this court head first,
of bleeding too much,

of not standing
when an officer stands on your feet.
You are falsely accused
of bearing false witness,
of reading between the lines,
of saying that a cat has nine tails.
You are falsely accused
of suffering persecution,
of fighting oppression,
of being beaten, hunted
and dragged down.
How do you answer these charges?

Fool   I am falsely accused.

Man   Then you are falsely condemned.

PART THREE – AN ENDING

Traveller 2   My God, help me.
My skull forms the frames
through which I see the world,
two bone frames
oval like Flemish mirrors.
I have been deceiving myself
all this while.
I am alone within a cage of bone.
I have no companions on this road.
I see two hands
moving before my face.
They are my hands, I think.

Traveller 3   They take the prisoner from that place
and to a place of execution,
and there they hang him by the neck
until he is dead.

Traveller 1   Until there is no life left within,
no mist on the glass,
no life left without.

Traveller 2   With each breath I take,
my ribs give little away.
With each breath
hands reach into my lungs
flexing and unflexing their fingers.
Do all the watchers on the hill
feel as I do now?

Traveller 3   I am strangely absent
as is a stranger's wont.
I lay my cheek against his foot,
bending my head to one side
as he once did.
The Fool is dancing in the air.
His dog waits in his shadow,
waits for a bone perhaps.

Traveller 1   The air is full of dancing feet,
of thump, of beat,
of angels,
weeping angels,
angels in fire,
angels carrying candles.
The world is destroyed at last.

Traveller 2   It is becoming very dark.
I cannot see the way
on the hillside
where no birds sing.

I know that I stand
at the crossroads,
for I have read the map
and my back is against the rood.
This much I know,
but as for the four roads,
as for the people
carrying their candles,
I do not see them.
There is no light in me

nor is there any
that reveals the hand of God
in this,
in this or in anything else.

Traveller 3   Our guide,
though tapping on our shoulders,
is absent.
He is dancing in air.

Traveller 1   Right now I want to wash his sweet feet,
to bathe the feet of the walker
in precious oils.
But all that bathes him is the rain,
running down his gaunt face,
mixing with the grime,
the blood, the saliva,
washing his white face.

Traveller 2   We must go from this place,
we must stumble on to the road.

Traveller 3   What road?

Traveller 2   Any road which will take us.

Traveller 3   The Fool must know the way –
he led us here.
Which way is he pointing?

Traveller 2   Up, down, what does it matter?
He is dead.

What does it matter which way
the hanged man faces?
He sees nothing.

Traveller 3   Nor do we
in this cursed darkness.

Traveller 2   Why did he lead us here
to crawl in candlewax?
Damn him!
Why did he lead us?

Traveller 3   Why did we follow?

Traveller 1   Because we had nothing better to do,
I think.

Traveller 3   No, no, because we believed him
though he spoke nothing
but riddles.

Traveller 2   What fools this fool has made of us!

Traveller 1   For me,
I would take the woman's part,
wash him and wrap him in linen,
in white linen.
Even now I trace my fingers
along the weft of it,
feel the slight imperfections.
In Damascus they sell it
by the yard.

Traveller 3   Like your shadow?

Traveller 1   It's all shadows here.

⚮

Traveller 1   Through briars we run
and gorse and bracken.

Traveller 3   And still we see nothing.

Traveller 2   We stumble through long grass –
grass which is folded
against the wind
making three blades
and all blades bite this day.

Traveller 1   Briars lash us,
whipping our bare legs.

Traveller 3   And still we run.

Traveller 2   All is dark and we are naked.

Traveller 1   What happened to our clothes –
my silks from the eastern markets?
Where did I lose them?

Traveller 3   Do not weep, my friend,
silks or rags are but masks

for our nakedness.
This dark will clothe us all alike.

Traveller 2   Why have you stopped?
Come! Come quickly!

Traveller 1   I've had enough of running.
In this darkness it is all one.

Traveller 3   Can't you see he's tired?
He's not as strong as you.

Traveller 2   See! I see nothing and nor do you.

Traveller 1   I must sleep.

‿❧

Traveller 1   What?

Traveller 3   Awake so soon?

Traveller 1   Have I slept so briefly?
Is it not yet day?

Traveller 3   If night has come and gone,
we have not noticed it.
If the sun has risen,
it has shed no light on us.

Traveller 1   It was a sleep that gave no relief.
I feel as if I have been on a long journey
not sleeping.

Traveller 3   And yet you slept deeply,
no shaking could wake you.
Once you cried out a question,
but not to us, I think.
Was there light in your dreams?

Traveller 1

I dreamt I was in a garden and the Fool was again our guide. His
rags were turned to a white gown. His hair, still unkempt, was
washed free of blood. His face, still thin, was smiling.

Although new to the place, I knew the smell of it to be that of
burning privet in my father's garden, of freshly made toast, of
the soap my mother used. I pulled the garden about me like
clean sheets. And the Fool led me through the many levels of the
garden, from stone terrace to the next. And as the Fool spoke to
me I heard laughter and weeping instead of words.

From one terrace he pointed out a great city that lay below us,
built on a bend of a steel grey river. And the city was familiar
and yet unfamiliar to me, with its spires and domes; the bridge
over the river had a double arch like the ventricles of a heart.
And the Fool began to lead me down into the valley through
poplar trees and past houses with lintels of painted wood and
window shutters like playing cards. Then at last we came to the
place where the city should have been, but we could not see it.
Instead the trees grew thicker and the path was besieged with

thorns. When the trees parted, we were in the bright light of a treefall. In the centre of the sunlight was an iron cage.

And in the cage I saw you, my friends, but the clothes you wore held only reflected colour, and your eyes were without light. And as I looked closely, I saw others in that cage, one on one, two on two, a dozen, a hundred, until I could not count them. And some I knew well, and some were strangers, and some were those people that one neither knows nor does not know. Some sat with their backs to the bars, heads in hands. Some crouched on the floor like caged beasts. Some stood reaching their thin arms through the bars, blindly opening and clenching their fingers.

"Can they see us?" I asked. "No," the Fool replied, and seeing the padlock open on the gate I said, "Shall we let them out?" "No, this is not the time," and he smiled. "Now you must go back," he said and placed his lips upon my forehead like ash.

Traveller 2   And? What happened?

Traveller 1   I woke.

Traveller 2   What are you talking about!
Come, now is not the time for sleeping.

Traveller 3   Why not? This is the darkest night
I've ever seen.

Traveller 2   Come!

Traveller 3   Go – leave us.

Traveller 2   Do not tempt me, I will.

Traveller 3   Do so.

Traveller 2   But we shall not meet again
in this darkness.
How will you follow?

Traveller 3   We will follow your blood
on the grass,
we will follow your fear
on the bracken.
These are the cords that bind us,
fear and wet blood.
And if you choose –
by these signs you will find us.

Traveller 2   Then I will go –
dragging you like a false trail.

Traveller 3   Well that's that.
The three are two now.

Traveller 1   Hold me in the darkness friend.
I want to rest my head on your breast.

Traveller 3   "Rock a bye baby on the tree top,
when the wind blows
the cradle will rock.
When the bow breaks
the cradle will fall,
down will come baby

cradle and all."

Traveller 1 I keep seeing the Fool
dragged by his feet
across the cobbles.
And everywhere they stopped
his head left a ring of blood.

Traveller 3 "Lully, lulla, thou little tiny child,
by by lully, lullay,
thou little tiny child,
by by lully, lully.
O sisters too
how may we do
for to preserve this day?
This pore yongling
for whom we do sing
by by lully lullay."

Traveller 1 And I see the woman lying
at the horse's hooves.
What's that?

Traveller 3 What?

Traveller 1 Over there in the darkness –
two spots of light.

Traveller 3 I see them –
moving through the blackness
towards us;
they're coming towards us!

Traveller 1	Shall we run?
Traveller 3	If we do, we lose our friend's trail.
Traveller 1	Stand it out then?
Traveller 3	Yes.
Traveller 1	Against our half-closed palms we feel the cold wet tongue.
Traveller 3	The Fool's dog is chewing on our fingers.
Traveller 1	What! Were we frightened of his eyes like the embers of Hell?
Traveller 3	Not I.
Traveller 1	Nor I.
Traveller 3	Hello boy, how are you then? Hey boy, you're as mangy as ever, but fat – he's been feeding you well in prison then – or have you been down in the Badlands searching for scraps?
Traveller 1	The Fool's dog drops his cargo of knuckle-bones upon the flags. He has carried his master's bones all this way

from the place of execution.

Traveller 3 I pick them up
and weigh them in my hand.
I place them
on the back of my hand
and throw.
I turn my hand to catch them,
all five.
I have my guide by the hand again.

Traveller 1 Give them to me – let me have a go.

Traveller 3 I do believe the mutt
has brought the sun with him.
Bird song
is beginning to disturb the dark.
The dog pricks up his ears.

෴

Traveller 2 I do not know,
I cannot say,
how long I ran
in that bleak night.
I stumbled and no hands held me.
The mire rose and stank around me
and my breath grew so loud
that I feared my ears would burst
with the sound of it.

And the storm that broke
upon the crossroads
and swept the hilltop
rode in my hair like a banshee,
striking my cheeks with her heels.

Woman   Holloo, holloo!

Traveller 2   Said the woman
twisting her fingers to the scalp.
And how I regretted
the loss of my friends
and my rash words.
I wanted to lie down, but my rider
held me in her tight thighs
and threw me on.
Holloo, holloo!

Woman   Woa!
Be still.
I have tossed you this night.
I have brought you
to the very edge of the sea –
the sinking of the world.
Can't you hear it?

Traveller 2   I hear nothing.
But I taste salt on my lips,
feel sea holly in my hand.
This sudden wind…

Woman   Rides up the cliff face.

Your night mare has brought you
to the very edge of dreams.
You wanted to lie down –
here you may fall
and need no rocking.

Traveller 2   I cannot see.

Woman   What does it matter?
The madman leads the blind.
I say to you the cliff is steep.
I say the sea is as angry as a milk pail.
I say blood is sweet
and death also.
Lay down your weary head.

Traveller 2   But if I lie down
I shall fall.

Woman   The sea is a dreaming
and death also.
Have you learnt nothing in your travels?
Don't you know the traveller's lore –
the next step will be your last?
Always we walk in darkness,
unless we take darkness by the hand.

Traveller 2   The next step I took
and fell into a deep sleep.

Traveller 2

I dreamt I was in a tall room. High on the walls ran a line of arched windows and through them came a daylight which served only to make parts of the room darker.

The Master said to us - "Make your beds and sleep."

Along the wall with their feet stretching into the room were rows of narrow beds. Without words we moved forwards, but each bed was so tightly packed against the other that we could not get our hands between them. I spoke to the others there, asking them to help me move the beds. But they looked past me as if they did not hear – or perhaps I was not there.

There was a grandfather clock at the end of the room which marked our vain efforts with its chimes. Slowly one by one the others gave up the attempt and lay down on the grey-brown coverlets and slept. The moon was now in the sky above the town and it slanted through the windows on to the faces of the sleepers. In its light and my gaze, they grew greyer and less distinct.

I could not sleep but climbing on to the bedstead and catching at the window frame pulled myself up to look out and across the silver roofs of the city, the domes and spires. Suddenly I heard music and over the roof-tops the Fool was dancing, whilst his dog clambered at his feet. I called out to him, and unlike the others he heard me and pressed his thin face against the pane. For a while his eyes seemed to be the eyes of the Master, but then they changed.

Abruptly my foot slipped on the metal bedstead and I looked down at the sleepers below me – they were no longer there. In the moonlight columns of dust swirled and danced. I felt faint and cried out to the Fool.

"You are near the surface, little worm," he said. "Reach out, it is not so far."

ৎৈৎ

Traveller 2   I pluck the feathers from my wings
and like a child say

Woman   He loves me, he loves me not,
he loves me, he loves me not...
(she continues as the other speaks)

Traveller 2   How perfect my feathers are –
white and fixed with wax.
The sun beats down.
(the voice of the woman breaks through)

Woman   He loves me, he loves me not.

Traveller 2   The sun beats down
tugging at my shoulder blades.
I have adorned my body
with down.
Dreams I have of falling –
so many dreams –

above me are the arms of children
soft skinned like the wind.

Woman   He loves me, he loves me not,

Traveller 2   And the pit is deep,
and the pit has many tiers.
Into the darkness,
oh lord of light,
I am coming.
I was falling and no one caught me,
I was flying and my wings were clay.

Woman   He loves me not.
Oh sons of Ler,
oh child of Leda,
where is your song?

Traveller 2   Where is your song?
With your wings you cover your mouth.
I fell through your arms,
I am falling into sleep.

Traveller 3   I see the world
as from a distance.
Is it spinning or am I?
I take my whip to it.
Spin little top,
you are my plaything now.

Traveller 2   Beyond the world is an absence –
a hole or a pit perhaps.

And the world is an absence
and the absence is in the world.
At certain points there is a hole in the ice.
It was at such a point
in the city of angels
that we slipped and fell.

Woman   He loves me, he loves me not,
he loves me.

Traveller 2   By the weir, where the children skated
on their blades of bone,
under the arches
and the stone angels
and George guarding the dragon
we slipped and fell
through the circle of candles.

ৎৎৎ

Traveller 3   We are come into that dark place
where All Hallows
is no longer celebrated,
and where we must pick up
our own shadows
from the mass of others
and carry them
over our forearms.
We are going into that dark house.

Traveller 2	I have forgotten that I was ever born.
Traveller 3	Under the portal, a lintel made of ash.
Traveller 2	Who are you – I do not know you? I have forgotten, I have forgotten the taste of bread, I am forgetting that I ever lived. Your faces are mist to me.
Traveller 3	But you must know us – we are your friends.
Traveller 1	You ate with us, you broke our bread, drank from fountains.
Traveller 3	A spider lay in the darkness it seems.
Traveller 1	You must know us.
Traveller 2	How can I know you? I have said your faces are nothing to me.
Traveller 3	What of the Fool? Surely you remember –
Master	Welcome gentlemen. Can I help you? I am the innkeeper and Master of this place.

PART FOUR – HELL AND BACK

Fool   You have passed through the doorway.

No voices now –
your tongues are split to the root.
I kiss your lips – they are whole again.
But still –
this is not a place for voices.
You have me by the hand, say nothing.
Watch everything, say nothing.
I will lead you.

I wear my kerchief of blood,
Margareta's pearls about my neck.
It is the mark of my departing.

Forgive me.
Forgive me for leaving you so.
Forgive me for leading you a dance,
my card was marked.
Forgive me, if my dance hurts you –
my back was broken.
If my head is crowned with blood and bells
you shall not bear it.
Forgive me.

May the servant be forgiven.
May the king wipe the feet of the travellers
and the prostitute lie with the queen of heaven.
Come, for I have much to show you.

And it will seem to onlookers
that all this while your body
struggled for air. But all you will know is
how very sweet it is – not to gasp.

Have faith my dear ones.
I shall not desert you even when you lose me.
Have faith.
For I have placed my mark on you.
It is in the eyes that you will find me.
When you shave,
the mirror will show you foolishness.
And men will laugh at you,
and women will hide their smiles.
Your children will have no respect for you.

This I have given you. For it is a truth
that when men see terrible things
they laugh.
And this is a terrible place.

Have faith.
I hold everything wrapped in my kerchief,
everything that is in the world.
For what is the world
but a string of bloody pearls?
And I lay them on the ground
to play marbles.

Traveller 2   Through many rooms

Traveller 1   we walked.

Traveller 3   At the end of each was

Traveller 2   a door

Traveller 3   and through that we saw

Traveller 1   another

Traveller 2   and another

Traveller 3   and another…
    (Traveller 1 & 2 continue)

Traveller 3   We were not sure if
    we walked through mirrors –
    each room was the same as…

Traveller 1&2   The other.

Traveller 3   It would seem that Hell
    is a museum.
    Each death a gallery of time
    made still.
    Pitiless the sound of feet
    on stone floors.
    The Fool's soft tread,
    our boots –
    pitiless in the quiet.

Fool	On your right –
Traveller 3	Our guide said.
Fool	On your right you will note the statues all in line. Dressed in mourning.
Traveller 3	Why do they mourn? Who would not mourn when all is still and redundant?
Fool	From the windows you will see the garden. Set out by the first gardener, the levels rise above the river. Each terrace – another bite of the fruit.
Traveller 1	Outside there was the sound of water,
Traveller 2	of birds,
Traveller 3	of laughter. Inside the constant tick of the clock, the mocking chimes, for hours do not pass here.
Traveller 1	Each mourner was lost to our passing.
Fool	They have been granted all their desires and found them wanting.

This is the ultimate hell – to look upon
yourself and find that you are hollow
and made of nothing.
Their hell is themselves: look on them
and weep.
Your weeping will not reach them.
If they were stone your tears might
wear a path into their hearts.
But they are conceits,
broken pots,
shadows.
Your tears will pass over them
and leave no stain.

Traveller 1   Tell us their history.

Fool   What do you take me for –
a poet?

Traveller 2   A fool.

Fool   Aha – there you have me,
by the hand as it were.

Traveller 3   You have not answered.
You have only questioned.

Fool   Isn't that my way?
What fool is it
who answers riddles?

Traveller 2   This is not a riddle.

Fool	No, this is the place that broke into your darkest dreams and you woke screaming. This is the place where all hope falters, where to breathe is pain.
Traveller 1	These two are indistinguishable. Like lava floes their forms combine. Their skin like cinder and their mouths like pumice.
Fool	Steam is their sigh; sulphur their laughter. Granite was their love; no pity etched in it, no seam of care; molten always and consumed. But here dust settles on the eyelids of the sleepers.
Traveller 1	Are they sleeping then? Do they dream?
Fool	Yes, of nothing. And that is the worst dream. It gnaws at hope like a rat.
Traveller 1	Do they dream of us?
Fool	Such vanity! I have said – they dream of nothing. Are you nothing then? No, they dream of nothing but themselves

and that is of nothing.
There is no hell greater than this.

The Master of the place wipes their brows
sometimes,
washes the floor, sweeps any leaves
that slip from the garden under the door.
Of course, they know none of this.

He keeps files on them all.
They are registered with numbered cards,
giving accession date, description of sin
and the place.
There is no end to the rooms here
and there is no end to the filing.

Traveller 2   But will you tell us their story?

Fool   Listen –

Traveller 3   He said and said nothing.

Traveller 1   So quiet –
absolute silence – like marble
but there are no veins
nothing to relieve the silence.

Traveller 3   I hear the rush of my blood
I hear the crunch of my ribs,
the flexing of muscles
to take in the air.
I hear the crash of eyelashes,

like the beating of waves;
like the suck of surf on shingle.

Fool   Your life is a tempest here.
The petrels career into the clouds.
They swoop over the foam.
They are buffeted. They call.
It is the scream of the damned.
Beneath them there are shoals.
Cast your nets on the starboard side,
there are lost souls for the taking.
Cast your nets on the port side
you will catch the silent roar of the depths.

Traveller 3   One among all those grey souls
seemed nearer to us
or we to him.

Traveller 2   Who is he?
His face is familiar.

Fool   It is as it should be.
Even if you had never looked at a history book,
your country's blood would cry out within you.
This is that man who held the world in chains.
At the brush of his pen, millions died.
At the sweep of his arm
babies burned.

Traveller 2   It is good that he is here.

Fool   There is no good here.

Traveller 1	Why does he weep?
Traveller 2	For conquest lost perhaps or lust unserved.
Fool	No, he weeps for paintings he did not paint.

و‌&حب

Fool	Come!
Traveller 1	The Fool was no longer beside us. Where was he?
Traveller 2	Where is he now?
Fool	Come. Reach up, it is not so far.
Traveller 1	Above us in a ring of light the Fool's face.
Fool	Enough is enough. You have seen enough. To go deeper would be to go too far. Even I cannot take you there. Once, for three days I walked the passageways, looked in cupboards, behind closed doors.

I put up warnings to the damned.
I walked unscathed in fire,
collected fragments of souls in my apron.
For three days and only three could I walk
and not fear.
I crouched on metal fire escapes
that climbed to nowhere,
I looked down into the depths
and felt the hot air on my face.
My hair shirt was made of asbestos
and my lung of iron.
And I dragged those that went before
into the garden and beyond.

I cannot tell you all that I saw
or all that I did.
But it grieves me to think of those
I did not save.

Come now away.

Traveller 3   He reaches down his thin arm
               and like a fisher
               hauls us through
               the circle of light.

Traveller 2   We stand blinking in the market square.

Traveller 3   At our feet
               the circle of candles burns.
               The red wax runs
               and marks our shoes.

Traveller 1   And the room is gone
and the museum
and the garden.
And the Fool is gone also.
Gone this time forever, I fear.

Traveller 2   Let us sit at the table
that overlooks the square.

Traveller 3   Let us drink coffee,
that strong black coffee
that marks the place.

Traveller 1   Let us put down our bags
and breathe the evening air.

Traveller 2   Let us play jacks
and the loser pays the tariff.
I have the bones.

Traveller 3   Who will start?

EPILOGUE

Traveller 3

My dear friends,
It seems so long ago, so very distant, our journey beyond the
bridge. And yet when the moon is high it weaves in and out of
my dreams like a dog through a fool's legs. I have often thought
to return, to go back to the city of angels and seek the cracking
ice. But the doormat needs beating or the hinges oiling, and the
intrusion of common things prevents my leaving.

I shall indeed set the pack on my back and begin again, but now
I am afraid. Our journey made me an exile in my own country,
always apart in some way, able most of the time to talk and to be
talked to, able to hold my son in my arms and trace myself in the
shape of his eyes. And yet I know myself to be not truly here. It
was a fearful journey, but I am sad that I have finished it, and I
am aware that I carry it with me now like a child's blanket.

You say that you have gone back to the city and all is changed,
that the angels are gone, the candles extinguished, that the
bridge is lined with trinket vendors and all is turned into
pettiness. That there is no dream within the dream, that there is
no dream at all. Forgive me if I cannot believe you. Last night I
heard the sound of dancing on the roof-tiles.

BACKGROUND

The poem was written following a visit to Prague immediately after the Velvet Revolution. A time which Zoe describes in her blog *Adventures in the Czech Republic:*

"My friend was renewing old acquaintances and exploring business opportunities and so I just took the opportunity in her absence to explore and soak in the atmosphere, and what an atmosphere it was. It is now hard to explain what it felt like back in early 1990. I had no guidebook and instead just walked, following my instinct, often going over the same ground time and again. I was completely breathless with the beauty of the place and felt the city's history – both glorious and sad – reaching out to me from alleyways and courtyards, through the railings of the Jewish quarter and from the facades of once rich buildings. Now the visitor finds the route from Charles Bridge to Town Square lined with hawkers, shops crammed with souvenirs and frankly often tat; then it was quiet and powerful. The statues on Charles Bridge stood alone and silent, without the accompanying flash of cameras and chatter of posing tourists.

On a number of occasions and at a number of places I came across small shrines of candles and flowers, set up to those who had been murdered by the oppressors. In Wenceslas Square there was a large makeshift memorial to Jan Palach – the student who had burnt himself to death in 1968 as a protest against the Russian suppression of the Prague Spring. Here there was a constant stream of people bringing flowers and lighting candles. It all felt hugely personal. I felt a voyeur watching the people's bowed heads. How could I comprehend what I was seeing? How could I share anything of the emotion that hung like incense in the air? And I was angered by other non-Czech visitors who stood around and took photos of it all.

I regularly made my way back to the lights and warmth of Cafe Slavia either to meet up with my friend or to drink black Czech coffee and eat the Cafe's rich cakes. Energy and wits refreshed; I would then venture back on to the streets. I do not know whether it was the caffeine or the intensity of emotion in Prague at that time, but I increasingly found myself unable to sleep. In that heightened state I found angels everywhere – statues, in frescos, in pictures. I sensed too, a presence in the air: the angels of Prague were weeping and rejoicing."

The poem that followed may have been inspired by that visit. It is not however about Prague. The city is in some ways a fusion of Prague and Istanbul, where Zoe had had another inspiring experience.

The Czech friend who features in Zoe's blog and who introduced Zoe to the Czech Republic was Hannah Kodicek. Hannah, who died in April 2011, was a multi-talented writer, actor and artist. In the latter part of her life, she was a story editor – working on the Oscar-winning film *The Counterfeiters* and advising on Danny Scheinmann's *Random Acts of Heroic Love*. Her monoprint used on the cover of this book was created by drawing with acrylic paints on glass and was in response to the poem.

ZOE BROOKS

After many years working with disadvantaged communities in London and Oxford, Zoe Brooks returned to her first love – writing and performing poetry, dividing her time between the UK and the Czech Republic. Her first visit to that country, only months after the Velvet Revolution, was a major inspiration for Fool's Paradise.

Zoe's collection *Owl Unbound* was published in 2020 by Indigo Dreams Publishing. Her poetry has appeared in many magazines and anthologies, including Michael Horovitz's *Grandchildren of Albion*, The Rialto, Pennine Platform, and *Magpie* - Roma Women's Poetry Anthology.